# CLASSIC CHINESE FURNITURE

*Classic Chinese Furniture: An Introduction*
Published 2001
Second Edition 2002
ISBN: 962-7283-43-6
Website: www.formasiabooks.com

© FormAsia Books Limited
706 Yu Yuet Lai Building
45 Wyndham Street
Central, Hong Kong

Written by Willy Lam
Edited by Nigel Cameron
Editorial assistance by Elizabeth Knight, Orientations
Designed by Format Limited, Hong Kong
Photography by Kwan Kwong Chung
Camera assistance by Sathish Gobinath
© Text and photographs copyright FormAsia Books Limited
Colour separations by Sky Art Graphic Company Limited
Printed in Hong Kong by Sing Cheong Printing Company Limited

FormAsia Books expresses its gratitude to the Hong Kong
dealers listed below for their participation and generous assistance
in compiling this volume.

**Altfield Gallery**
3rd Floor Prince's Building
10 Chater Road
Central, Hong Kong

**Artemis**
46 Wyndham Street
Central, Hong Kong

**China Art**
15 Hollywood Road
Central, Hong Kong

**Chine Gallery**
42A Hollywood Road
Central, Hong Kong

**Andy Hei Ltd**
22nd Floor Oriental Crystal Commercial Building
46 Lyndhurst Terrace
Central, Hong Kong

**Hobbs & Bishops Fine Arts**
28 Hollywood Road
Central, Hong Kong

**Honeychurch Antiques**
29 Hollywood Road
Central, Hong Kong

**The Red Cabinet**
Shop No. 5, Chinachem Hollywood Centre
1-13 Hollywood Road
Central, Hong Kong

**Zitan Oriental Antiques**
Yu Yuet Lai Building
45 Wyndham Street
Central, Hong Kong

---

*All rights reserved. No part of this publication may be reproduced, stored in or introduced into a retrieval
system, or transmitted in any form or any means (electronic, mechanical, photocopying, recording or
otherwise) without the prior written permission of the publishers of this book.*

# Classic Chinese Furniture

## An Introduction
WILLY WO-LAP LAM

FormAsia

*The outer court of an 18th C. Guangdong official's home with classic Guangdong-style blackwood chairs, altar tables and screens.*

**Tools of the Trade** *Carpenter's planes for all-round work with cross-handles slotted into a groove behind the plane, and rabbet-planes. Chinese carpenter planes are pushed away from the body and held by the handle if they have any, or else held with one hand at one end and the other near the opposite end.*

# Classic Chinese Furniture

## An Introduction
### WILLY WO-LAP LAM

The well-known French critic, Odilon Roche, once wrote of furniture from the Middle Kingdom as a celebration of "simplicity, nobility and grandeur". For the Chinese historian Wang Shixiang, these eminently useable *objets d'art* were paragons of "purity, dignity and gravitas". The finely crafted chairs, coffers and cupboards have a Confucianist air of propriety about them. The pulse slows when one is seated on a Ming dynasty horseshoe back chair.

Classic Chinese furniture is today enjoying a strong revival of interest, both in Asia and the West. Though remaining eminently functional, chairs, coffers and cupboards are essentially works of art; a testament both to the natural beauty of wood grain and the understated elegance that can be achieved through contours and ornamentation.

What a triumph for the modern notion of economy of style and function! The most elegant of chairs are unupholstered. Their form tends to encourage the adoption of an upright posture. And indeed, what better manner could there be to slip into the Taoist way of simple commerce with nature as the seasons scroll past? And perhaps, reclining in a canopied bed with lattice work and flowing silk, one may begin to daydream like the Chinese philosopher Zhuang Zi, of man metamorphosing into a butterfly.

While the quasi-art objects are a testimony to eclecticism,

the best works are harmonious marriages of the *yin* – the natural beauty of the wood grain – and the *yang*, the design and ornamentation. The vast range of classic Chinese furniture remains overwhelming. Collectors' items range from brushpots, cosmetic boxes and side tables to gilded wardrobes, lacquered cabinets and imperial thrones.

Consider for example a screen room divider (page 128) that consists of panels, each of which bears different inlaid carvings. In the way of *trompe l'oeil*, it's a virtual landscape within the living room: or the detailed apothecary's cabinets (pages 26, 34 and 44) which boast tens of small drawers each engraved with descriptive characters for the herbal remedies they contain.

The resplendence of Chinese furniture lies in the marriage of design, elegance and simplicity with detail. How does one ensure that each wood-grain pattern of the door panels of a cupboard or wardrobe perfectly matches that of its neighbours? One can lose oneself admiring the carvings alone, which come in free style, relief or openwork. Apart from floral and mythical creatures such as dragons and phoenixes, engravings on screens and cabinets often feature scenes from novels such as *Romance of the Three Kingdoms* and *Tales from the Western Chamber*. A simple brass locket, lock-pin or lock-plate can be geometrically intriguing. Even the miniature metal handles for opening drawers can be ornaments in their own right. Restraint in all things is one of Chinese furniture's essential strengths.

Most classic Chinese furniture is fashioned of wood, which in itself has reverential connotation and a historic vibrancy in Chinese cosmology. After all, Chinese call old trees *shen mu*, or God's wood. It is a tribute to the versatile skills of carpenters and artists that their stock-in-trade ranges from oak, elm, cedar, cypress and camphor to pine, teak, walnut, and mahogany.

The cognoscenti favour the prized *huanghuali mu* (yellow flower pear wood), *jichi mu* (phoenix tail or chicken wing wood) and *zitan mu* (dark-purple sandlewood). *Huanghuali* is a yellowish rosewood with fine and subtle markings that was the revered wood of Ming dynasty craftsmen. *Jichi* is so called because of a feather-like grain that enhances the sheen and splendour of the phoenix's plumage. Many Qing dynasty palace items were made from this rarity.

*Zitan*, an extremely-hard rosewood which became largely extinct by the early Qing dynasty, lends itself to intricate, multi-faceted carving. This is despite the fact that the wood is so dense it sinks in water. In historic times *zitan* and *huanghuali* were as costly as gold and gems. Lately new *zitan* woods to replace those sources in China which had been exhausted have been discovered in Indochina, and Burma.

Many Western connoisseurs have a preference for lacquered or otherwise painted (pigmented) furniture of a more colourful and elaborate design. In recent decades, however, relatively plain hardwood products have found favour with both collectors and habitual users. For variety, post-Qing dynasty and contemporary furniture makers are increasingly turning to bamboo and rattan, or combinations of disparate materials.

Chinese furniture as we know it did not come into being until the

Tang dynasty (618 – 907 AD). Before that, Chinese knelt or sat cross-legged on woven mats surrounded by sparse, low-level furnishings. Chairs, stools, tables and the like are believed to have been introduced from neighbouring countries in the wake of the migration of cultures and religions, particularly Buddhism. Art historians tend to the opinion that in terms of style, if not technique, furniture design and carpentry were firmly established during the late years of the Song dynasty (960 –1279).

Furniture became a true art form of great purity in the Ming dynasty (1368 – 1644).  The finest Ming examples are celebrations of classic line and understated elegance. Yet chairs, chests and cupboards from this period sometimes exhibit elaborate inlaying and lacquer coatings with engravings and paintings. The canopy beds of the literati were used not only for sleep but for conversation and discussion. Antique Ming furniture is now vastly expensive, much prized by collectors and exhibited world-wide in great museums.

In the Qing dynasty (1644 –1911) there began a shift of taste to more opulent ornamentation. Artisans serving the Emperor Qianlong (1736 –1796) added new motifs with subtle Western influences. One of the best examples of the sumptuous Qianlong period is the emperor's rosewood throne, now in the T.T. Tsui Gallery of London's Victoria and Albert Museum. This red-lacquered throne displays minute carvings of cloud-like emblems, flora and fauna, and historical personages in an elaborately sculptured panoply.

It was also during the Ming and Qing periods that carpenters and particularly cabinetmakers perfected ingeniously designed ways of joining wood. Strong, reliable glue had not yet been discovered so most Ming furniture was bonded by distinctive mortise-and-tenon joints or wooden pegs traversing the intersection. Allowance was made for shrinkage so that the items  strengthened in time and in use. Such techniques probably coincided with the prosperous Ming construction of palatial homes in cities and coastal areas such as Suzhou and Wuxi. The import of hardwood varieties from Southeast Asian countries encouraged novelty and experimentation in the furniture métier.

Talented carpenters from various regions began to establish distinctive provincial styles. Naturally, the affluent Shanghai-Jiangsu region excelled in opulence and variety of style, but pleasant surprises could be discovered in the hinterland. Shanxi became famous for well-preserved ancient formats as well as slightly garish red and black lacquerware. From Tibet came furniture incorporating Buddhist and other spiritual objects.

The great Ming and Qing designers and craftsmen, like China's great potters, were and have remained unsung heroes. In China, there are no named masters of carpentry comparable to Boulle of France, or Thomas Sheraton and George Heppelwhite of England. Early literature on the subject of furniture is rare. The carpenter's talent and ability did not rate as an art form.

The Chinese tradition of ignoring the achievements of the craftsmen who created and made great furniture in the past, continued after the 1949 Communist revolution. During the years of communal chaos between (1966 and 1967) numberless Ming and Qing screens, tables, chests and chairs were either destroyed or burned for fuel. Except for a traditionally negligible minority of intellectuals, household furnishings did not enter the category of art. Not until as late as the 1980s was that age-old trend reversed.

Today the best accessible locations for the appreciation of classic Chinese furniture are the world's great museums. The Victoria and Albert in London comes to mind as does the Museum of Classic Chinese Furniture in Renaissance, California and the Metropolitan Museum of Art, New York. (See also page 150 which lists prestigious museums with substantial collections of classic Chinese furniture). In China itself, as a consequence of traditional uncaring and later thoughtless depredations, there is only a limited amount of great classical furniture available to be viewed. In the Forbidden City – The Great Within – or *Tai Nei* as it used to be termed, is a minimal display of furniture. More examples are available in the great houses of the past in the provinces, for example at Suzhou. In Taiwan in the well-known Lin residence at Taichuang and in the Cheng residence at Hsinchu, furniture of the traditional Fujian provincial style has been preserved in pristine condition. Sadly, little else in China has survived the centuries.

Chinese furniture first found international status through the activities of Western scholars, connoisseurs, collectors and plunderers. In the destruction of the Summer Palace and Yuanmingyuan near Beijing in 1860

what appears to have been all but the entire furnishings of the palaces was looted by the marauding armies of the Western powers. It is in very large part these and later loot from another Western raid in 1900 to suppress the Boxer Rebellion, which form the core of the Chinese collections in Western museums today. The 1930s traveller Peter Fleming in his book *The Siege of Peking* commented: "Looting went on squalidly for months, with each nationality blaming some other for setting a bad example and claiming that its own hands were clean."

As a result by the 1930s and 1940s the collection and study of Ming and Qing furniture had spawned a body of Western experts. European, and increasingly Japanese dealers were in Beijing, Tianjin and Shanghai, eagerly tracking down furniture and purchasing from households which had connections to the Qing dynasty and its court circles. Yet another source was missionary, diplomatic and expatriate families who far-sightedly had begun accumulating furniture in the early years of the 20th century: much of this, after the Communist revolution, came with them to Hong Kong and so onward to the West.

By the late 1970s Chinese furniture began to be accorded the scholarly attention and status that had long been lavished on Chinese ceramics and painting. And two decades later in the 1990s the prices of quality Chinese furniture began to set records at Sotheby's and Christie's.

A sound horseshoe back armchair of Ming vintage could command as much as US$100,000. A *zitan* long table with intricate flower carving was sold for more than US$350,000.

The question was then asked: are these prices sustainable? The answer appears to be probably in the affirmative. One reason is the quite limited numbers of fine examples likely to come on the market. The other potent reason relates to the intention of *nouveau riche* Chinese mainland collectors who readily will fly to New York or London to attend auctions when truly fine items of exquisite furniture become available.

There is one salient difference in the study of Chinese classic furniture that separates it from the study of Chinese paintings and ceramics. Authentication is often problematic. Despite the recent tightening-up of customs supervision on the Chinese side of the borders, fine furniture still emerges. What muddies the picture somewhat is the reconstruction of whole pieces from parts of several items, some of which may be genuine Ming or Qing, or perhaps not.

Today there are many factories in Qingdao, Panyu and Guangdong capable of reproducing commendable look-alikes for increasingly interested affluent Chinese patrons who aspire to the status of possessing what to them represents Ming or Qing furniture.

To meet the increasing interest in the knowledge of Chinese furniture of this comparatively recent range of collectors, connoisseurs and the uninitiated enthusiast, articles in scholarly and semi-scholarly journals appear with mounting frequency and books are published, by spirited amateurs, knowledgeable furniture dealers and dedicated scholars.

**Previous page:** *Bronze locket traditionally cast with lotus motif corners.* **Left:** *Red lacquered, square corner painted cabinet embellished with gold leaf. Early 19th C. Elmwood. Shanxi Province.* **Below:** *Red lacquered wedding cabinet. 19th C. Northern Elmwood. Ningbo Province.*

*Compound clothing cabinet of two sections. Upper cabinet can easily be treated as an independent item of furniture.* **Right:** *Circular brass lock plate with three pear-shaped handles. (The pear in China symbolizes fortune and prosperity).*
*18th C. Huanghuali wood. Beijing. Hebei Province.*

**Left:** *Red and black lacquered low storage chest on horizontal platform. 19th C. Ju Mu (Elmwood). Suzhou Province.* **Centre:** *Leopard legged cabinet with circular brass lock plate. 19th C. Walnut. Shanxi Province.* **Above:** *Gently tapered book cabinet. 18th C. Jichi Mu (Chicken wing wood). Beijing. Hebei Province.*

# 24 CLASSIC CHINESE FURNITURE

*Two black and red medium size cabinets decorated with landscape motifs. 19th C. Elmwood. Shanxi Province.*

*Forty-five drawer herbal medicine cabinet with original paper labelling in place. 19th C. Cedar wood. Hebei Province.*

**Left:** *Cabinet with 'tiger skin' door panels and bat motif brass lockets. In China the bat with its embracing wings is emblematic of happiness and longevity. 19th C. Cedar wood. Fujian Province.*

*Book cabinet with bronze door locket. Rodded sides and doors. Late 18th C. Cedar wood. Shanxi Province.*

**Below:** *Waisted side-cabinet in original red lacquer finish. Northern Elmwood.* **Lower:** *Small, two-door red lacquered cabinet. Zehjiang Province.* **Right:** *Red lacquered tapered cabinet. Late 18th C. Southern Elmwood. Zhejiang Province.*

**Previous pages:**
*Detail of a forty-eight square-drawer herbal medicine cabinet. 19th C. Elmwood. Shanxi Province.*
**Below and right:**
*Wardrobe with ornately carved doors with vase and floral motif. Brass lock plate with vase motif latch. 18th C. Huanghuali wood. Shanxi Province.*

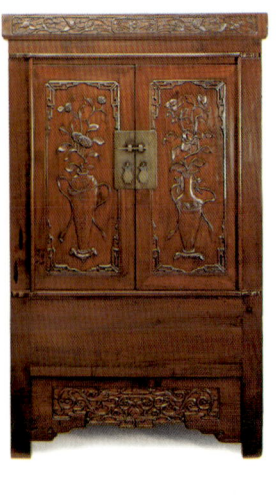

**Left:** *Lacquered black and red cabinet with gilt decoration on face and apron. Late 18th C. Ju wood. Shanxi Province.* **Below:** *Red lacquered wedding cabinet with copper gilt decoration. 18th C. Elmwood. Shanxi Province.*

**Below:** *A pair of display cabinets with carved openwork railings. (Wan motif). Late 18th C. Ju wood. Shanxi Province.* **Right:** *Detail of square-cornered black lacquered cabinet with circular lock plate. 19th C. Elmwood. Shanxi Province.*

**Left:** *Wardrobe with white copper bi-tone hinges and locket. 19th C. Blackwood. Guangdong Province.*
**Right:** *Book cabinet. 18th C. Jichi Mu (Chicken wing wood). Guangdong Province.*
**Below:** *Cabinet with white bronze hinges and locket. Late 18th C.* Huanghuali *veneer on elmwood. Beijing. Hebei Province.*

*An apothecary's cabinet with forty-five drawers with original labelling. Mid 19th C. Ju wood (Elmwood). Suzhou – Hangzhou.*

*One of a pair of red lacquered two-door chests, embellished with twelve floral panels, four of which are black lacquered. Late 19th C. Cedar wood. Zhejiang Province.*

**Below:** *Two-door black lacquered cabinet. 18th C. Elmwood. Shanxi Province.* **Right:** *Square legged cabinet with caned door panels. 19th C. Yang wood. Hebei Province.*

**Left:** *Kitchen cabinet with front and sides constructed of vertical rodding. 19th C. Cedar wood. Anhui Province.* **Below:** *Shanghai scroll cabinet with separate upper and lower portions. Lower segment constructed with removable front panel. 19th C. Cedar wood. Anhui Province.*

**Below:** *Low cabinet with two drawers and two doors. Copper handles and locket. 19th C. Walnut. Shanxi Province.* **Right:** *Red lacquered wedding cabinet with large circular lock plate. (Basket-shaped openers, symbolic in China of fruitfulness.) 19th C. Camphor wood. Shanghai. Jiangsu Province.*

**Previous pages and below:** *Black and red lacquered low chest with gilt painting. 18th C. Elmwood. Shanxi Province.* **Right:** *Red lacquered square-cornered cabinet, decorated in gold leaf with hand painted motifs of landscapes, pomegranates and butterflies. 19th C. Elmwood. Shaanxi Province.*

*Square black lacquered clothes cabinet with* **(right)** *classic yellow brass locket. Late 18th C. Elmwood. Shanxi Province.*

60  CLASSIC CHINESE FURNITURE

*Red lacquered wedding cabinet decorated with lotus and butterfly motifs in gold leaf. 18th C. Ju Mu (Elmwood). Zhejiang Province.*

**Below:** Brass-fitted seal chest with seven drawers and hinged top, made for Western export market. 19th C. Huanghuali wood. Hebei Province. **Top right:** Jewellery box with brass locket, hinges and handles. 19th C. Huanghuali wood. Hebei Province.

*Rural household sideboard with four drawers and decorated hardware. 19th C. Elmwood. Shanxi Province.* **Right:** *Tapered two-door book cabinet with burlwood door panel sections and brass lock plate. 18th C. Huanghuali wood. Beijing. Hebei Province.*

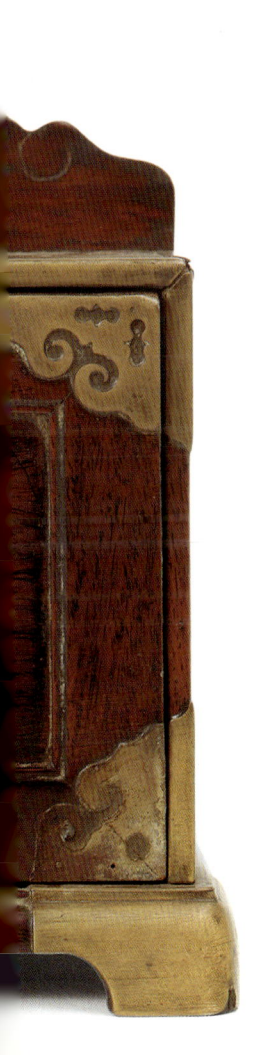

**Left:** *Seal box, face, frame and base mounted with bi-tone hardware. Late 17th C.* Huanghuali wood. Hebei Province. **Top:** *Storage/stationery box with brass lock plate. 19th C.* Elmwood. Beijing. Hebei Province. **Above:** *Three-tiered picnic box carved with dragon motif. Mid 19th C.* Blackwood. Beijing. Hebei Province.

**Below:** *Carved rectangular storage box with engraved hardware. Early 18th C. Zitan wood. Hebei Province.* **Right:** *Box with brass fittings. 18th C. Huanghuali wood. Shanxi Province.*

**Main picture:** *Long side-table with single plank top. Side panels with stylized dragon motif. 18th C. Walnut. Shanxi Province.*
**Below:** *Altar table with bridle and tenon joint. 19th C. Top surface camphor and Cedar wood combined. Fujian Province.*

**Right:** *Doctor's desk. Two pedestals with drawer and two shelves, support a single table-top plank. 19th C. Iron wood. Beijing. Hebei Province.* **Below:** *Three part scholar's desk with four-drawer top supported by two-side pedestals each with a drawer. Early 20th C. Iron wood. Shanghai. Jiangsu Province.*

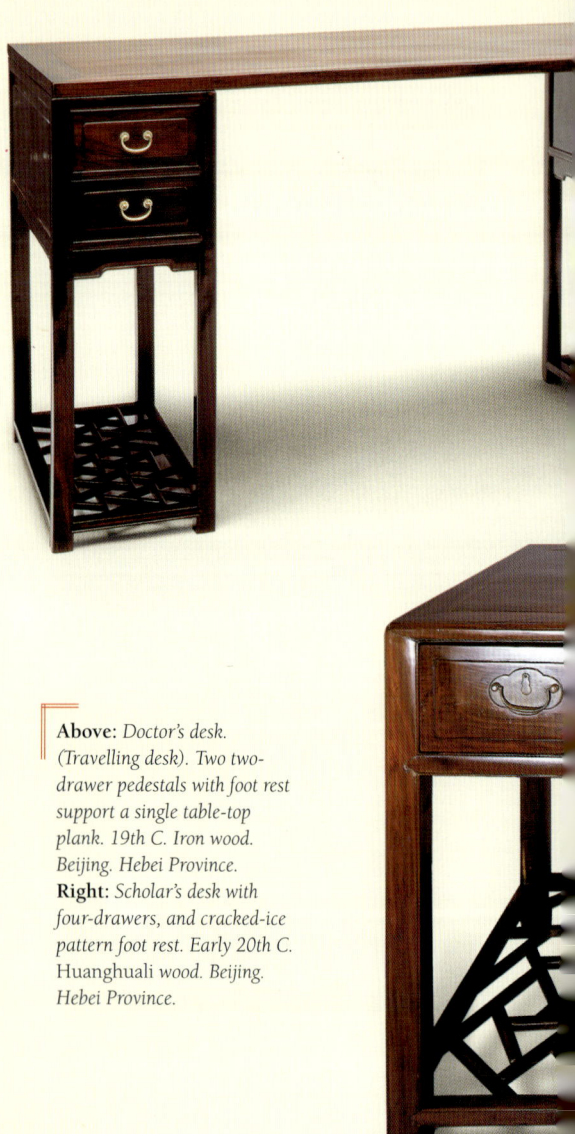

**Above:** *Doctor's desk. (Travelling desk). Two two-drawer pedestals with foot rest support a single table-top plank. 19th C. Iron wood. Beijing. Hebei Province.*
**Right:** *Scholar's desk with four-drawers, and cracked-ice pattern foot rest. Early 20th C. Huanghuali wood. Beijing. Hebei Province.*

**This page and lower right:** *Square incense table with extravagantly curved legs. 18th C. Yu Mu (Elmwood). Shanxi Province.*
**Top right:** *Square incense stand. 19th C. Lichi wood. Fujian Province.*

**Right:** *One of a pair of supports for a trestle table stand with carved panels. 17th C.* Huanghuali *wood. Shanxi Province.* **Below:** *Country wine tables, one with open wood grain. 18th C. Elmwood. Shanxi Province.*

**Top left:** *Round-legged side table. 18th C. Huanghuali wood. Hebei Province.* **Top right:** *Lacquered two-drawer coffer with inverted ends, which doubles as an altar table. 19th C. Elmwood. Shanxi Province.* **Main image:** *Altar table with archaic dragon design on apron. 19th C. Elmwood. Shanxi Province.*

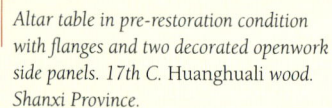

*Altar table in pre-restoration condition with flanges and two decorated openwork side panels. 17th C. Huanghuali wood. Shanxi Province.*

*Lacquered altar table with thick floating top panel. Carved openwork on the side panels. Early 19th C. Elmwood. Shanxi Province.*

**Right:** *Wine table/side table. 18th C. Huanghuali wood. Beijing. Hebei Province.*
**Below:** *Ming-style altar table. Early 18th C. Iron wood. Beijing. Hebei Province.*

*Sideboard with deep relief carving. Two lower drawers conceal secret compartment. 18th C. Elmwood. Shanxi Province.*

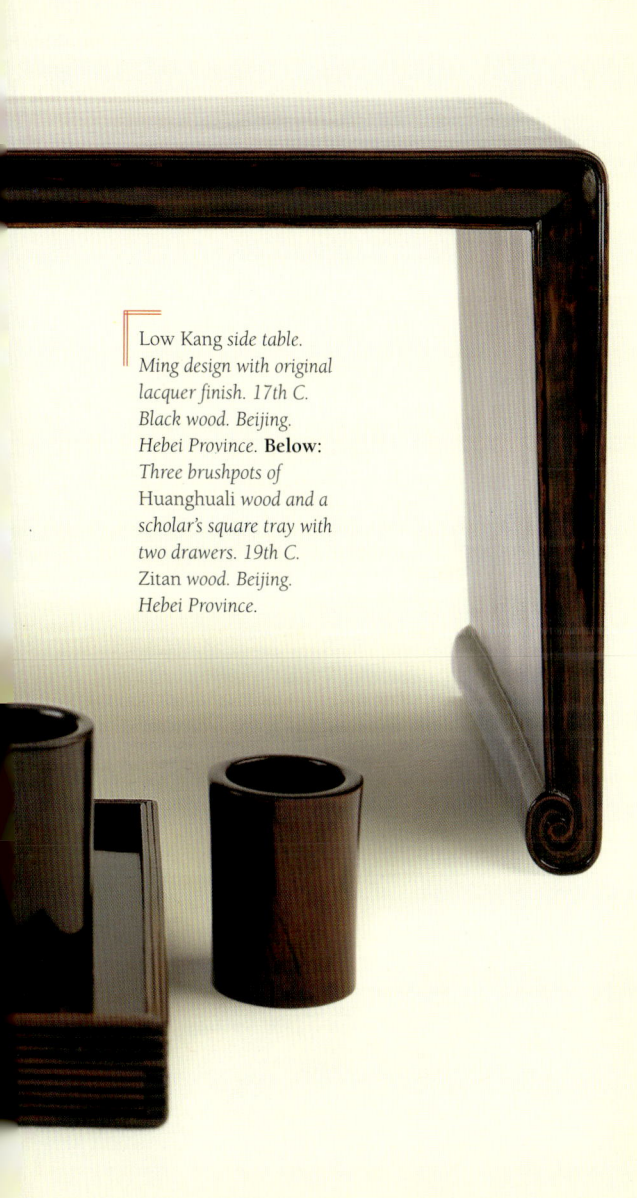

Low Kang *side table. Ming design with original lacquer finish. 17th C. Black wood. Beijing. Hebei Province.* **Below:** *Three brushpots of Huanghuali wood and a scholar's square tray with two drawers. 19th C. Zitan wood. Beijing. Hebei Province.*

**Below and right:** *Wide altar table. Rosewood. Reproduction. Jiangsu Province.*

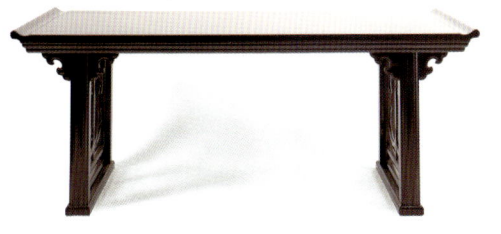

*Elaborately embellished small side table. Mid-Qing Dynasty. Yu wood. Shanxi Province.*

Red lacquered, rattan-topped low table with two drawers. 19th C. Elmwood. Zhejiang Province.

*Lacquered three-drawer table, with latched middle drawer. 19th C. Elmwood. Shanghai. Jiangsu Province.*

Three classic Ming-style side tables. 18th C. Huanghuali wood. Beijing. Hebei Province. **Lower right:** Table with hump back stretcher. 17th C. Huanghuali wood. Beijing. Hebei Province.

*Horseshoe back armchair in pre-restoration condition with double medallion on back splat. Late 17th C. Blackwood. Shanxi Province.*

Lady's daybed with scrolled legs and revolving headrests at both ends. 19th C. Blackwood. Suzhou Province.

**Left:** *Beijing official's hat style armchair with curved back splat. 18th C. Elmwood. Shanxi Province.*
**Below:** *Southern official's hat style armchair with vase and floral design carved on back splat. 19th C. Elmwood. Shanxi Province.*

*Open-grained opera bench with naturally inclined 'C' curve. 18th C. Elmwood. Shanxi Province.*

**Left:** *Lacquered northern official's hat style armchair with cane seat. Late 18th C. Elmwood. Shanxi Province.*
**Below:** *A pair of northern official's hat style armchairs with cane seats. 19th C. Elmwood. Shanxi Province.*

**Below:** *Two folding yolk-back chairs with hawser seat.* **Right:** *Detail of back splat. 18th C. Yu wood (Elmwood). Shanxi Province.*

*Mahjong table with chairs. Carved apron with imitated bamboo design. Table top with folding legs. 18th C. Blackwood. Shanghai. Jiangsu Province.*

**Left:** *Horseshoe style armchair with carved dragon motif on back splat. 18th C. Elmwood. Hebei Province.* **Below:** *Southern official's hat style armchair with carved back splat. 19th C. Elmwood. Hebei Province*

**Below:** *A pair of Rose (Wenyi) chairs with opaque brown/red lacquer finish. Late 18th C. Elmwood. Shanxi Province.*
**Right:** *Southern official's hat style armchair. Back splat with openwork. Open grain seat. Early 19th C. Cedar wood. Hebei Province.*

*A pair of horseshoe back armchairs with decorative back splat and cane seats. Late 18th C. Elmwood. Shanxi Province.*

**Left:** *High yolk-back armchair with cane seat. 17th C.* Huanghuali *wood. Shanxi Province.*
**Below:** *A pair of horseshoe back armchairs with dragon carving on back splat. 19th C. Blackwood. Beijing. Hebei Province.*

*Summer daybed with railing on three sides. Bed surface of bamboo slats. Early 19th C. Elmwood. Shanxi Province.*

**Left:** *Southern official's hat style armchair with openwork back panel and apron. 19th C. Elmwood. Zhejiang Province.*
**Top:** *Horseshoe back armchair. 18th C. Blackwood. Hebei Province.* **Above:** *Southern official's hat style armchair with curved back splat. 19th C. Blackwood. Hebei Province.*

*Part of a six-panel screen with open fretwork carvings. Central reliefs depict lotus and water lilies. 19th C. Elmwood and fir. Suzhou Province.*

**Left:** *Three-tiered kitchen cabinet. Livestock were stored in the lower two compartments. 20th C. Bamboo. Taiwan.*
**Below:** *An asymmetric display stand. 20th C. Bamboo. Zhejiang Province.* **Bottom:** *Slender, clothing cabinet. 20th C. Bamboo. Jiangsu Province.*

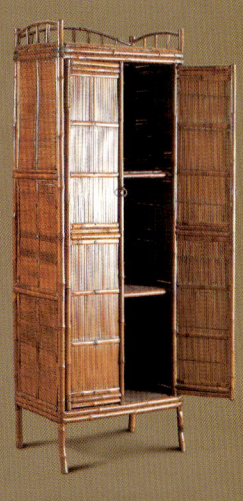

**Right:** *A kitchen cabinet with three separate storage areas decorated with folk medallions. Clasp carved in the shape of a fish, (symbol of abundance in China). 20th C. Bamboo. Zhejiang Province.*

*Two kitchen cabinets.* **Below:** *Ventilation slats for two lower compartments permit air circulation for livestock. 20th C. Bamboo. Fujian Province.*

**Below:** *Low table with fine geometric design openwork apron and woven rattan inset. Contemporary. Bamboo. Fujian Province.*
**Right:** *Black lacquered waisted hoof foot recliner with slatted surface. 19th C. Bamboo. Shanxi Province.*

*Three country chairs of varying size and design. Contemporary. Bamboo. Zhejiang Province.*

**Right:** *Low table with rattan surface. Contemporary. Bamboo. Fujian Province.* **Below:** *Children's stroller and high chair. Contemporary. Bamboo. Zhejiang Province.*

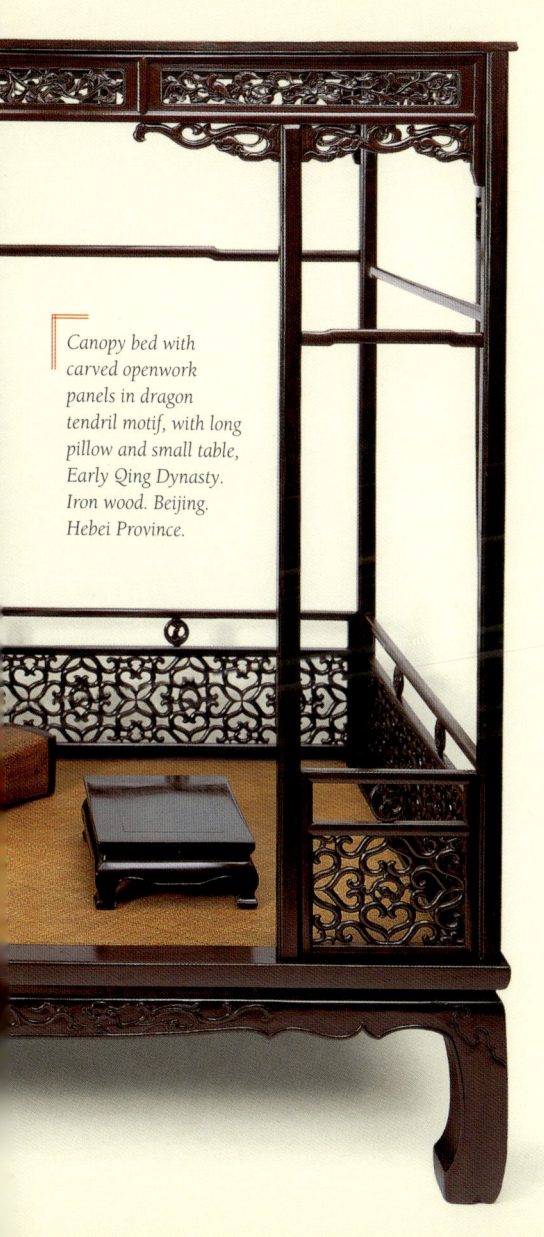

*Canopy bed with carved openwork panels in dragon tendril motif, with long pillow and small table, Early Qing Dynasty. Iron wood. Beijing. Hebei Province.*

Luohan bed with carved apron and sides with low relief Chinese characters for blessing, longevity, health and peaceful death. Early 19th C. Elmwood. Shanxi Province. Accessory: Woven rattan double-pillow, elegantly concave form.

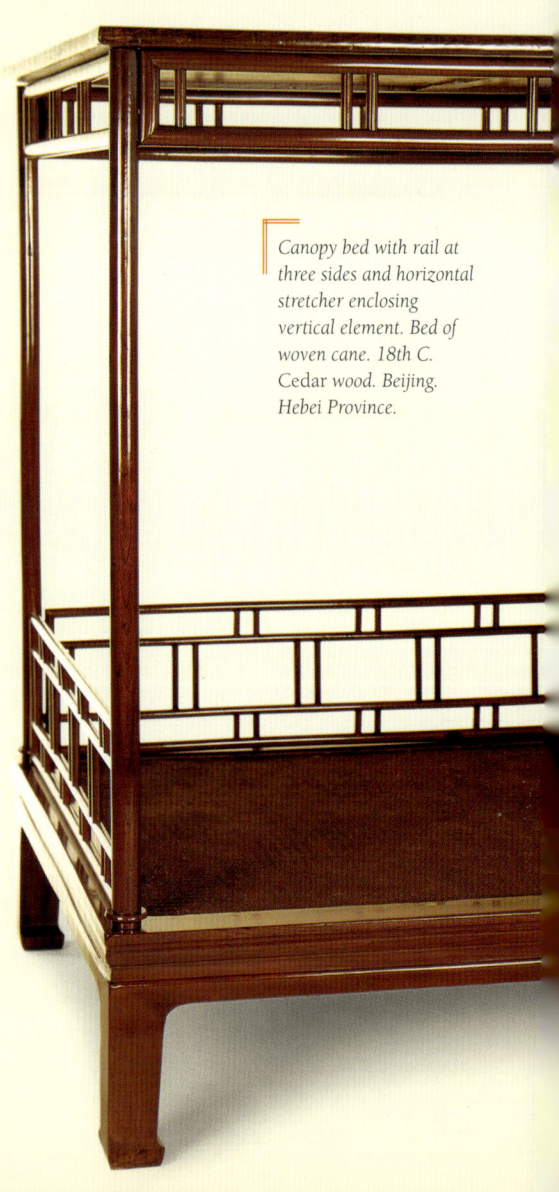

*Canopy bed with rail at three sides and horizontal stretcher enclosing vertical element. Bed of woven cane. 18th C. Cedar wood. Beijing. Hebei Province.*